FEB 83

PICTURE AMERICA

PICTURE AMERICA

JIM ALINDER: PHOTOGRAPHS
WRIGHT MORRIS: WORDS

ANSEL ADAMS: INTRODUCTION

New York Graphic Society Books

LITTLE, BROWN AND COMPANY

BOSTON

First edition

LIBRARY OF CONGRESS CATALOGING IN PUBLICATION DATA

Alinder, James.
    Picture America.

    "A New York Graphic Society book."
    1. Photography, Artistic.   2. United States—
Description and travel—Views.   3. Alinder, James.
I. Morris, Wright, 1910–   .   II. Title.
TR654.A483   1982   779'.997392   82–8008
ISBN 0–8212–1502–7   AACR2

Designed by Susan Windheim

Typeset in Sabon by The Stinehour Press
Printing by Gardner/Fulmer
Bound by A. Horowitz and Son

New York Graphic Society books are published by Little, Brown and Company.
Published simultaneously in Canada by Little, Brown and Company (Canada) Limited.

Printed in the United States of America

For Mary

ACKNOWLEDGMENTS

The photographer would like to acknowledge generous grants from the National Endowment for the Arts and from the Woods Foundation, which were important to the making of these photographs. For their significant help with this project, thanks to Ansel Adams, Mary Alinder, Robert Baker, Debbie Bradburn, Phyllis Donohue, David Featherstone, Jo Morris, and Chris Rainier.

INTRODUCTION

Seldom have I seen two superior creative people join their efforts and produce a result as rewarding as this book. Jim Alinder's discerning eye and Wright Morris's prophetic poetry grasp moments of beauty and surprise in the simplest passages of American life. In these pages, life abounds. We are nourished by the compassionate curiosity of the photographer's incisive vision and the writer's selective reincarnation of experience.

I have photographed mostly in the creative euphoria of the natural environment in the West as a matter of choice and circumstance. Much of what I know of Middle America is from photographs of it. Unfortunately, many of the photographs of our vast America, of its urban, suburban and countryside areas, dwell on the ironic concepts of visual blight, poverty of human spirit, and the desolation of humanity. It seems "correct" to see America's slums and highways this way. There is little joy and no love left; mostly pollution, ugliness, and depression. We know there is more. Jim Alinder's photographs penetrate this common stereotype. They give us a loving, yet balanced and questioning report on the most recent decade in our history. Wright Morris's characteristically peerless style provides an equivalent experience.

Alinder's photographs embrace the common evidence of our society, revealing with clear delineation the nature of both our urban and rural scenes. The chaotic "familiar" becomes the particular "reality." His pictures evidence no doctrine. They convey the assurance of a participant in this American life of ours, a participant with a perceptive eye and an inclusive heart. Possessing both direct vision and democratic mind, he has made these beautiful photographs with a Kodak Instamatic camera on Verichrome Pan film packaged in a plastic cartridge, the same materials available to anyone at the corner drugstore. Never have I felt the medium to have been better served than it has been here by Alinder, with a camera usually dismissed as only being good for the quick, easy snapshot by the inexperienced amateur.

Approximately one-third of these photographs were made in Nebraska, which was Morris's birthplace and has continued to serve as the location of many of his novels. It is also where Alinder worked for ten important, creative years. America's heartland, too often seen through a plane window, is caressed in this volume. While the photographs clearly cluster in Nebraska, they also extend from coast to coast. During the years just before and after the American Bicentennial, Alinder traveled the length and breadth of our country documenting his response with his Instamatic. He moved to California in 1977, thus many of the later photographs were made in that state.

Morris's literary passages, written to accompany each specific photograph, are priceless fragments of the flavor of America. They are to be savored, these quips and slivers of remembered conversations, reflections, penetrations and bits and pieces of experience that the photograph has served to unlock from his memory. Time has distilled his expression into essence. These excerpts of life, from a master of incisive writing, have the authority that only wisdom and compassion can reveal.

Respecting the essential purity of both photography and writing, I am wary of the usual photo/text volume. There have been few successes. I am most fond of *Time in New England* with Paul Strand's great photographs subtly related to texts from the pens of early New England essayists, poets and preachers, ably selected by Nancy Newhall. Also outstanding are the earlier books of photo/text by Morris, particularly *God's Country and My People*. The Alinder/Morris pairing works because each of the contributions retains the personal style of the artist, and each is supreme in quality. Alinder's images do not illustrate the text, nor does Morris's text "explain" the pictures. The words and photographs complement each other. Two expressive entities combine to form a third. There is no obscurity, no conceptualized morass, no concession to the trite rituals of style and content.

In the face of the banality I find in much of contemporary art, the work of these gifted artists emerges as a beacon. Alinder and Morris have given us important moments in the life of our people. Here the commonplace is truly uncommon. Here is creative magic.

ANSEL ADAMS
Carmel, California

PICTURE AMERICA

"Look what's happened, you kids, in just your grandaddy's life-time —"

They said, "Is Laramie where we eat?"

He said, "You know what a dirt road is? You know what a gravel road is? A dirt road is mud up to your axle, a gravel road chews up tires and spits out rubber. Between here and North Platte your grandaddy had three blowouts, and they were flat all around, not just on the bottom. Your grandaddy had to pump it full of air and then tighten up the lugs. Even your daddy could do all that, and jack up the car, when he was no bigger than you are. How about that?"

They said, "Is there a McDonald's in Laramie?"

Population growth, Laramie, Wyoming

First it was just open country, with some sheds for chickens and a clearing where they had a few cows tethered, then the kids had a sandlot over in one corner, then came the big parking area for the rigs and trailers with the neighbors complaining about the idling engines, then there was all this talk about who would trouble to drive so far out in the country just to do a little shopping. What happened next you can see for yourself.

Pioneers Blvd. at 48th Street, Lincoln, Nebraska

Why is it the doors always open the wrong way? I ask him. I can't get over how different it looks until they build it, with a roof on it, and windows you can measure. All of that is just for the garage? I ask him. If cars belong in the house, let him live in them. It's going to seem strange not having any neighbors but he says they'll be there before I hang the curtains. With the kitchen where it is I won't see most people until they knock.

New construction — Kirkwood Drive, Lincoln, Nebraska

Most of the people I know who built their own houses have had nothing but headaches. How do you know what you want till you see it? Until they've learned how to build it, and repair it, you've no guarantee it'll work. Arnold says a good tract house is one they've got the bugs out of, like a good used car.

Back in Elgin we had everything we could ask for but nice winters and cable TV, both of which we now got.

—

Tract homes, Sun City, Arizona

During the Paleolithic period there were no wheels at all, and their use was not known to the American Indians.

But all that has changed.

Sidewalk and vehicles, Lincoln, Nebraska

The bounce of balls on the backboard. The dribble on the concrete. The hooting and yelling. The swish of the net and the long-awaited silence.

In the silence we note how little time it takes small boys to grow up big.

Garage with buckets, Pebble Beach, California

The kids love it, I think Estelle loves it — the kids aren't underfoot all winter — but anyone who has to work inside, like I do, sitting in a room with the blinds drawn, you begin to lose track of time passing. Now some people like that. Other people get the feeling life is passing them by.

Handprint, Pacific Grove, California

If I told mother that we had to sit here by the ocean with our sweaters on, to watch the fireworks, she would just know we were crazy. What else can you expect of people who live where the earth shakes, as she says.

Fireworks and palm, Pacific Grove, California

There's baked heart and dressing today, that's the blue plate
special.
The breaded veal cutlet is nice. Or the chicken-fried steak —
How about a couple of eggs, sunny side up?
Hash browns or french fries?
Make it the french fries.
Anything to drink?

Restaurant facade, rural Nebraska

They could make us all tires that would never wear out, as well as matches that would relight. They could even make light bulbs that would never burn out, but you know what it is them rascals really want?

They want to keep us in the dark.

Politician's booth, City Park, Lincoln, Nebraska

I like the flowers all right but what I don't like is to see them in a pitcher without any water.

The White House, Washington, D.C.

We shop at K Mart, don't we, Mom?
Yes, dear, but we don't eat there.

K Mart Family Picnic, Pioneers Park, Lincoln, Nebraska

Before Mother was married she lived in Cody and Daddy was a brakeman on the Burlington Railroad. The train often had to stop because of the buffalo crossing the tracks. It wasn't unusual, in a bad year, for Indian squaws to come to her back door and ask for food. The men would starve before they'd beg, but they'd eat what the women provided. They weren't all friendly. I guess they just about scared Mother to death.

Pioneers Park, Lincoln, Nebraska

It seems more like yesterday Daddy drove us over to Wichita where we had a Chinese dinner then went to a double feature movie. But Jane has never stopped being her mother's girl, have you, hon?

Main Street, Laverne, Kansas

The child sleeps. Nothing could be simpler. For an instant only, we experience a time that is not registered in countdowns, then with a shrug, and a shame-faced smile, we tiptoe away and let the child sleep.

Baby in basket, Racquet Club, Carmel Valley, California

Silent snow, secret snow, falling softly, impartially, on fields and highways, on streets and byways, to be tracked and patterned by creatures and small fry, soon clogging the streets, stalling the traffic, lowering a curtain through which lights glow and flakes fall big as feathers, dampering the harsh metallic scrape of shovels, the *slap-slap* of chains. Under the snow the rock salt nibbles away at the ice.

Snowstorm, 22nd and "O" Streets, Lincoln, Nebraska

She thinks about the golf course backed up to the privy and how as she got older she was ashamed to use it, and would squat in the weeds. She thinks of heartbreak and the *whoosh* of the fire when her daddy poured coal oil on it, and lit it, and she thinks of the long, long wait for the kettle to boil. She thinks of flies floating on the dipper of water and the drip of clothes drying in the kitchen. As old as she is, as idle as she looks, she thinks day and night of the way it once was, of what she alone remembers, but she cannot bear the thought of where it will all go when she dies.

Entering "It's a Small World," Disneyland, Anaheim, California

We were in Spain in April — I think it was April — then we went to Sicily and the isles of Greece. Don't you just love Greece? We've both got so we eat so little what we look for is nice background music. We like it better than talk.

Statues with view, restaurant entrance, Florida

After seeing Lon Chaney in *The Phantom of the Opera* I moved from the sidewalk to the center of the street and ran like the wind for safe harbor.

That was real terror. REAL terror is always stamped Made In Hollywood.

Jaws in drydock, Universal Studios Tour, Los Angeles, California

"You kids see that? You don't see that every day."

"Who was it, Mommy?"

"Just a lady in a buggy."

"Don't she have a car?"

"She doesn't want a car. What she wants is a horse and buggy."

"Why can't we have one?"

"Your daddy can't afford a horse," she replied.

On the road, Lancaster County, Pennsylvania

We planned this trip for almost a year, and what does she do? She forgets her medication. She might as well not go to bed at all without it. There's worse things, Grandma, my oldest tells her; what if we'd come off without our camera? Why, I guess I'd rather not be here at all than see it all and not have our own pictures.

Mount Rushmore, South Dakota

Deep in the heart of Texas, signed and dated by those who found it, a Cadillac, having fallen from Grace, has a new career as an identified object.

The first of ten half-buried Cadillacs, Amarillo, Texas

The first thing you've got to do, to get a handle on something, is give it a name. Hurricanes have names. Whose idea was it to give them the names of girls? We're great at giving names to anything big and noisy. Take the name *Little Boy*. The first time you hear it it seems an odd name for a bomb, but you get used to it. You've got to save Big Boy for the BIG one, right? The kids have a ball around here, it's like a park, and if they're ever going to get a handle on the future . . .

Atomic Bomb Museum, Los Alamos, New Mexico

I don't see a thing. Now why would they do that?

Idea was to get you to look. You can get people to look if you put a frame around it.

Listen to Mr. Know-it-all, she said.

They wouldn't say it was there, if it wasn't.

Oh, wouldn't they? I'll believe it when I see it. I don't see a thing.

Picture spot, Great Meteor Crater parking lot, Arizona

PICTURE SPOT
MT. HUMPHERY
HIGHEST POINT IN ARIZONA

"Here's Gossage, folks. Listen to that ovation! He's coming in to face Brett who's 3 for 4 this afternoon. I suppose we could say, beyond fear of contradiction, that Gossage is the premier of great relievers — the way Lite is the premier of light beers. Lite gives cool satisfying relief of thirst the way Gossage gives quick satisfying . . ."

Pacific beach, Pacific Grove, California

Say we agree on a 3-for-1 stock split. I know, I know, but say we just agree on it?

There's a call for Mr. Purvis —

I'll take it. Excuse me.

Lovey, this is Miriam —

What did I tell you?

You said not to call you.

I'm on top of this deal, but if you want me to blow it just go on calling me here at the club.

Private party, The Lodge at Pebble Beach, California

PRIVATE PARTY

The scenic prop is stopped time.
The storage is a time capsule.
The blur of time that passes is you, the viewer.

Prop storage, Universal Studios, Los Angeles, California

You folks from Ohio? My oldest girl is in Akron. She says the schools are closed more than they're open. She finds the winters colder than they are out here, at least she notices it more. If you're in or around Akron, and would like a bite to eat where you can come as you are, try the Prairie Diner. You can see it from the freeway, if by now they haven't turned it into something else.

Service station, Interstate 80, Nebraska

When I was a boy the people next door strung a wire around the yard to keep us kids off the grass. Later they put up a fence, with a gate, and then they got a big dog. Over the long summers, when the windows were open, we could hear their daughter play the piano. She stopped, when she got tired of just playing for herself. When I came back from college they had fenced in the porch, and made it part of the house. Nobody seemed to know who the daughter had married, or who bought the house. When we get what we want we often find we don't like it, or we get too much of it, or we find we can't afford it. How do you know, when you begin, if you're keeping people out, or fencing them in?

Fence and iceplant, Pacific Grove, California

He walked from the house to the car in the morning, and from the car to the porch in the evening, where he sat on the steps to read the newspaper. In August he drove his mother to see her people in the Ozarks or visit with her daughter in Beatrice. Every three or four years he bought a new used car. He sorted mail on the train between Lincoln and Denver, but he could use his rail pass to go most anywhere he wanted. But he preferred to drive. He said he felt more at home behind the wheel of a car than he did in the house.

House and car, Lincoln, Nebraska

Fact is, we don't really know what He looked like. He was in his early thirties. Think of what He did! All over the place, and most of it on foot. I suppose that's why we think of Him as older. A boy Ellie knew used to look just like Him. Long hair, and beard, liked to run around barefoot. I used to wonder what it was he had on his mind.

Store window, St. Petersburg, Florida

She's got the TV, and friendly people to talk to, some of them from Polk and Seward, but she's been her own person for so long, by herself, she just can't seem to adjust to people. She won't eat unless they bring it to her, off by herself.

House, bush, snow, Lincoln, Nebraska

Smooth as glass, slick as ice, fast as greased lightning, sharp as a razor — but where the devil is the waxed bread paper?

Slide, Dennis the Menace Park, Monterey, California

Barbara and Ann both walk to school, can you imagine! No busing, no hoodlums, we just can't believe it! Charles doesn't much like the climate, but when we think of the children — and my God, what else is there to think of?

New elementary school, Lincoln, Nebraska

Along with our Cheerios we begin the day with a picture of a picture, a complex media message that combines how we see with what there is to be seen, the camera's eye both before and behind the one that we turn to the world.

Stieglitz' "Steerage" on TV at breakfast, Lincoln, Nebraska

Arthur said: I get this offer to make the move to California, one Louise has always wanted, and we can't make it. A three-bedroom house runs about two hundred and fifty grand. You know what the interest is on two hundred and fifty grand?

Louise said: Don't leave that extension cord where Jimmie will find it! You remember what you said about mowing on Sunday? When you two great minds are ready we'll eat — Arthur, you hear me?

Summer conversation, Ypsilanti, Michigan

Skyscapes are replacing landscapes, for the airborne, just as in-scapes are replacing skyscapes. What better props for our daydreams than clouds, the escape hatch for those whose minds are elsewhere.

Somewhere over America

We think of heat, of languor, of pleasure, of vacation, of cooling creams, Visa cards, and faraway places. Finally we think of what we'd rather not think of, and then we get to thinking that maybe we've had enough. The best and worst thoughts come later, when we can't sleep.

Afternoon at the pool, Yosemite National Park, California

It's hard to take a bad picture. The directions say so. You just aim the camera, and press the button. Later, when you get the prints, you can see that it's the angle that counts.

Photographing, Aspen, Colorado

It's not that I mind the heat so much, I told him, but when the wind blows just to be blowing, not to spin any wheels or do anything useful, just to give me wrinkles and splitting headaches, I could scream. If it's not nailed down out here, it blows away — and I'm not nailed down.

Plains wind, Lincoln, Nebraska

Smiling and waving, the Pork Queen signals the conversion of corn into pork, and the triumph of beauty over the dustbowl.

The triumph of the chauffeur is that of one who gallantly sits and waits.

Fourth of July parade, Seward, Nebraska

Nebraska
Pork Queen
LaJean Novak

What's your name, son?

Jesse.

Jesse what?

Jesse King.

The way you got that balloon tied to you, if a wind came along
you'd fly off with it. How would you like that? You wouldn't like it,
would you. You got to watch what it is you tie yourself to, don't you?

Watching Fourth of July parade, Seward, Nebraska

It was along through here, you know, they used to run the cattle, the long-horned critters, lean and mean as weasels. The Chisolm Trail is just there, west of the new freeway — and all the way north to the railroad at Salina, Kansas. You know what it was that put an end to all that? Rolls of barbed wire.

Historical marker, Fort Worth, Texas

Your Uncle Fred liked to wear his sporty hats at the table, with his coat off, which I got tired of but he didn't. He just loved hats. If it was a straw he liked to tilt it, which I suppose was what he liked about it. He didn't like caps. He would let his ears freeze just to wear a hat. He had some for the winter, some for the summer, and a green fedora he kept for Sundays. He used to keep a dollar in the band to make sure he would have it for the collection. If he went to Omaha he usually came back with a new hat. He took it personal when Clyde and Avery refused to wear one. When he passed away your Aunt Mae found that he had more hats than she did. Some he never wore. If I was going to take a picture I would ask him to take off his hat, so we could see him better, but the ones with a hat on look more like him, a toothpick in his mouth.

Hat display, Neiman-Marcus, Dallas, Texas

When I think what it was like! How we didn't burn the house down with the needles on the rug and the dripping candles! If I had a choice between all these presents and a white Christmas, I'd take the white Christmas. I'll never get used to the carols without the snow. But don't tell him.

Christmas tree and gifts, Sun City, Arizona

The truth is I don't like it much the way it is, but I like it better than the way it was. I can sell it right now for enough to retire on. That's progress. Ain't it?

Parking lot, Sun City, Arizona

It's just hard to believe, but you can see his father in almost everything Leonard does. Ronald is more like me, he wants peace in the family. Leonard is orderly. I'd like to save whoever marries him some of the things I've learned in eighteen years with his father but it don't seem to matter how much you've learned there's just so much you can tell anybody, if you can tell him anything.

Backyard toys, Aspen, Colorado

FOR SALE

Three bedrooms, two and one-half baths, den, fireplace, wall-to-wall carpets, large level lot, near shopping and schools.

Back porch, backyards, Lincoln, Nebraska

John Wayne, John Kennedy, Martin Luther King, Robert Kennedy, Jimmy Carter, Jerry Ford, Richard Nixon, Lyndon Johnson, Hubert Humphrey, Dwight Eisenhower, Harry Truman, George Wallace, Nelson Rockefeller, Jacqueline Kennedy, Ronald Reagan, Lady Bird Johnson.

If the dollar is now worth 30¢, and falling, how long before all of us are in shadow?

Famous Americans adorn dollars, Times Square, New York, New York

I can't stand crowds of people, I simply *hate* football, all this hooting and yelling gives me a headache, but in three years we've only missed one home game. Why do you go? Floyd asks me. You want to know why? I stop just being me.

University football game, Lincoln, Nebraska

She reads — "This chick with her suntan oil, her beach towel, her rubber volleyball and her radio, came along the beach at the edge of the water where the sand was firm. Soft sand shortens the legs and reduces their charms, as you may know. This one pitched her camp where the sand was dry, slipped on one of those caps with the simulated hair, smoked her cigarette, then . . ."

Sunbath, reading, backyard, Fresno, California

If I could come again it would be as a fish. The kids would love it! Why do you suppose they feel so good in water? It's more supportive. Air is too thin. If there's water up to your chin, and it's warm, you really feel safe and protected, back where you came from.

Hot tub after birthday party, Pebble Beach, California

He said, It looks like a Christo.

She said, What's a Christo?

How about that, he said, she don't know about Christos.

What it *really* looks like, she said, is a dream, gift wrapped.

Whose dream? he said.

Your dream, she said.

Show car, before show, Sun Valley, Idaho

Along the way role-playing, with models and products, and in this moment of stopped time, between the foreground and the background, there is a new time that has duration, an after-image of the figure, the face averted, that persists long after we have stopped looking.

Along Madison Avenue, New York, New York

Clearly the music hath charms, and the charm of it lies in how well it served the differing dancers, blowing an old flame into new life, or luring new life into the future of heart's desire.

New Year's Eve, December 31, 1979, California